A Look At...

Inventions and Discoveries

WORLD
BOOK

www.worldbook.com

Staff:

Executive Committee

President
Jim O'Rourke

Vice President and Editor in Chief
Paul A. Kobasa

Vice President, Finance
Donald D. Keller

Vice President, Marketing
Jean Lin

Director, Human Resources
Bev Ecker

Editorial

Director, Digital Product Content
Development
Emily Kline

Editor
Kendra Muntz

Manager, Indexing Services
David Pofelski

Manager, Contracts & Compliance
(Rights & Permissions)
Loranne K. Shields

Digital

Director, Digital Product
Development
Erika Meller

Digital Product Manager
Lyndsie Manusos

Digital Product Coordinator
Matthew Werner

Manufacturing/Pre-Press

Manufacturing Manager
Sandra Johnson

Production/Technology Manager
Anne Fritzinger

Proofreader
Nathalie Strassheim

Graphics and Design

Senior Art Director
Tom Evans

Coordinator, Design Development
and Production
Brenda B. Tropinski

Senior Cartographer
John Rejba

Book Design by
Matt Carrington

Senior Designer
Isaiah Sheppard

World Book, Inc.
180 North LaSalle Street, Suite 900
Chicago, Illinois 60601
USA

For information about other World Book publications, visit our website at www.worldbook.com or call 1-800-WORLDBK (967-5325). For information about sales to schools and libraries, call 1-800-975-3250 (United States), or 1-800-837-5365 (Canada).

Library of Congress Cataloging-in-Publication Data
Inventions and discoveries.
     p. cm. -- (A look at …)
   Includes index.
   Summary: "An introduction to inventions and discoveries from ancient to modern times, including how they were developed and their effects on society. Features include fact boxes, illustrations, period photographs, a timeline, a glossary, and a list of recommended books and websites" --Provided by publisher.
   ISBN 978-0-7166-1790-7
   1. Inventions--History--Juvenile literature.
I. World Book, Inc.
T15.I5775 2011
609--dc22
                                    2011006434

A Look At …
Set ISBN 978-0-7166-1786-0 (print)

eBook editions:
ISBN: 978-0-3324-2 (EPUB3)
ISBN: 978-0-7166-1781-5 (PDF)

Printed in China by Shenzhen Donnelley Printing Co., Ltd.
Guangdong Province
2nd printing August 2016

Picture Acknowledgments:

The publishers gratefully acknowledge the following sources for photography. All illustrations and maps were prepared by WORLD BOOK unless otherwise noted.

Front Cover: Shutterstock

Bernie Epstein, Alamy Images 41, BibleLandPictures/Alamy Images 12, Chris Hellier, Alamy Images 38, ClassicStock/Alamy Images 47, Dennis Hallinan, Alamy Images 4, Geoffrey Kidd/Alamy Images 12, GL Archive/Alamy Images 58, Goddard Automotive/Alamy Images 31, Lebrecht Music and Arts Photo Library/Alamy Images 24, Mary Evans Picture Library/Alamy Images 26, 30, 35, 37, 41, 44, North Wind Picture Archives/Alamy Images 7, 14, 20, 26, Paris Pierce, Alamy Images 17, Photo Researchers/Alamy Images 9, Photos 12/Alamy Images 20, The Print Collector/Alamy Images 26, 42, World History Archive/Alamy Images 10, 22; Art Resource 22, 23; Bettmann/Corbis 30; David Sarnoff Library, Princeton, NJ 48; Don Di Sante 36;Andreas Rentz, Getty Images 54, Bridgeman Art Library/Getty Images 57, Christian Science Monitor/Getty Images 45, Frederick Church, George Eastman House/Getty Images 36, Gabriel Bouys, AFP/Getty Images 53, Hulton Archive/Getty Images 6, 16, 40, 43, 46, Lambert, Archive Photos/Getty Images 48, Popperfoto/Getty Images 46, Ryan Anson, AFP/Getty Images 52, Sankei, Getty Images 49, Science & Society Picture Library/Getty Images 21, 28, 32, 33, 34, 38, 52, SuperStock/Getty Images 28, Time Life Pictures/Getty Images 14, Walter Sanders, Time Life Pictures/Getty Images 39; dpa/Landov 45, 60; Library Of Congress 50; Mary Evans Picture Library 6, 8, 11; Illustrated London News Ltd/Mary Evans 32; Cusp and Flirt/Masterfile 5, V&A Images/Masterfile 16; NASA 50, 61; Shutterstock 4, 5, 13, 16, 19, 34, 36, 42, 54, 56; imagebroker/SuperStock 59, Science and Society/SuperStock 10, 18, Underwood Photo Archives/SuperStock; U. S. Air Force 9

CONTENTS

There is a glossary on page 62. Terms defined in the glossary are in type that looks like this on their first appearance on any spread (two facing pages).

Introducing Inventions and Discoveries

Inventions and discoveries have changed people's lives throughout history. Many of the things we use every day—this book included—are the result of thousands of years of invention and discovery.

Invention or discovery?

When something that already exists in nature is noticed or recognized for the first time, we call it a discovery. Many discoveries are made by scientists. An invention is the creation of something that never existed before. For example, when early peoples saw natural forest fires burning, they discovered fire. They learned how to make their own fires by using a burning branch to light a pile of dry sticks. Later, people invented matches and other ways of making fire. Look around and you will see inventions everywhere.

Many inventions develop over time. In about 1500, Leonardo da Vinci drew a design for a helicopter-like flying machine. The first piloted helicopter flight took place in 1907, but a stable, practical helicopter was not built until the 1930's.

Changing our lives

Thousands of years ago, people lived by hunting animals and gathering wild plants. To find food, they had to move from place to place. About 9000 B.C., people began to grow their own crops and raise such animals as sheep, goats, and cattle. They had invented farming and no longer needed to wander in search of food. Now people could settle in villages.

Much later came the **Industrial Revolution** of the late A.D. 1700's, with such inventions as the **steam engine** and new machines for use in factories. The Industrial Revolution brought another great change in the way people lived, as they moved from farms to the cities to work in factories. Change still affects our lives today as we move through the communication revolution.

Many inventions have given us control over our environment and helped us to live better, easier, and happier lives. If we could not invent, we would be at the mercy of the climate and the land. Inventions have enabled people to survive the hazards of the environment and develop a civilized society. People continue to invent and discover to solve the many problems that the world faces today.

Good or Bad?

Many inventions have made life better for people. But some, such as weapons of war, have been harmful. Other inventions have had both good and bad effects. The automobile, for example, has:

- given people a fast, convenient means of travel.
- created jobs for many workers.
- hurt and killed people in traffic accidents.
- jammed city streets.
- contributed to air pollution (dirt and waste).

Typewriters were developed in the late 1800's. Beginning about 1980, personal computers and printers began to replace typewriters for home and office use.

Why People Invent

People invent things for several reasons. Some inventors are driven by curiosity. Others have an urge to create. Still others hope to make money. Most inventions are created to satisfy the needs of people.

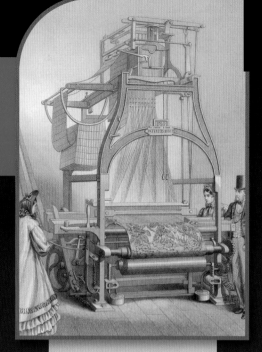

The flying shuttle loom was developed in the 1700's. On machines like this, weavers could weave cloth much faster than before.

Three basic needs lead to inventions and discoveries. They are economic needs, military needs, and social needs. An economy is a system of managing the production, delivery, and consumption of goods and services. Let's look first at examples of how economic needs can inspire inventions.

Demand speeds supply

Before the age of factories, individuals made most manufactured goods. For example, weavers and spinners made cloth in their homes. They worked by hand and at their own pace. Merchants bought cloth from these home workers.

By the early 1700's, merchants wanted more cloth to meet growing demand. In 1733, John Kay, an English clockmaker, invented a weaving machine called the flying shuttle. With this machine, weavers could make cloth faster than the spinners could provide them with thread. Cloth merchants then had to hire more spinners, or find a new, faster way to spin thread.

During the 1760's and 1770's, three Englishmen—James Hargreaves, Richard Arkwright, and Samuel Crompton—invented machines to help spinners work much faster. Now there was more thread available than there were weavers and weaving machines to make cloth. In the mid-1780's, Edmund Cartwright, another English inventor, invented a steam-powered weaving machine, or loom. At last, weavers could keep up with the spinners.

Before the age of factory machines, textiles were generally made in small home-based textile shops.

Mr. Whitney's cotton gin

Steam-powered weaving machines provided great amounts of cloth at lower cost. Merchants could sell cloth at lower prices, so people bought more. Because of this, the demand for raw (natural) cotton increased, and a new problem arose.

Raw cotton contains seeds that must be removed before the cotton can be used on spinning machines. Picking out the seeds was done by hand, a process that moved too slowly to keep pace with the new demand for cotton. In 1793, the American inventor Eli Whitney built a machine called the cotton gin. One cotton gin could remove cottonseeds as fast as 50 people working by hand. Now the cotton growers could keep up with the spinning and weaving machines. One invention had spurred another, and then another. And people's lives greatly changed.

Eli Whitney

As a teenager, Eli Whitney (1765-1825) set up a nail-making business. While studying to be a lawyer and doing odd jobs to earn his keep, he heard cotton growers complain that they could not make money because of the time it took to clean the raw cotton. So Whitney invented his famous machine—the cotton gin. He could not make his machines fast enough to meet the demand. Other people copied the idea, and he took them to court to try to protect his invention. He later made muskets and other weapons for the United States government.

The cotton gin saved workers the task of removing cottonseeds by hand.

Over the centuries, war and the threat of war have driven people to create new and ever more destructive weapons. Military needs have led to many inventions and discoveries.

Gunpowder and shot

Soldiers in ancient times fought with swords, spears, and bows and arrows—weapons that changed little over hundreds of years. A great change came in the 1200's with the use of gunpowder in war. People in Asia were probably the first to discover that a mixture of charcoal, the mineral saltpeter, and the chemical element sulfur produced an explosive black powder. This knowledge moved westward and eventually changed the face of war in Europe. The stone walls of castles were no defense against rockets and cannon balls fired by gunpowder.

The Gatling gun of 1862 had several barrels spun by turning a handle. In 1883, American-born inventor Hiram Maxim made the first fully automatic machine gun.

Gatling gun

Maxim gun

What Was Greek Fire?

Greek fire was a chemical mixture first used in warfare in the A.D. 600's. It burned furiously, even in water. Warriors in the Middle Ages (A.D. 400's through the 1400's) shot Greek fire with arrows and through tubes. No one knows for sure how it was made, but it probably contained liquid petroleum (oil) thickened with a sticky natural substance called resin and the chemical element sulfur.

Ancient Chinese warriors fire gunpowder rockets in battle.

World War II fueled the development of bigger and faster airplanes, such as the American B-24 Liberator bomber. After the war, the eventual application of jet engines to passenger aircraft made air transportation available for the first time to large numbers of people.

◀ An atomic bomb explodes over Hiroshima, Japan, on August 6, 1945. Since World War II, nuclear weapons have not been used, but technology behind them has resulted in the widespread use of nuclear energy.

Two world wars

New weapons that appeared during World War I (1914-1918) included the airplane and the tank. In addition, the Germans proved the submarine's effectiveness as a deadly warship. A one-man submarine powered by a hand-cranked propeller had been used in the American Revolution (1775-1783), but it failed to sink a British warship in New York Harbor.

During World War II (1939-1945), scientists invented the atomic bomb, the single most destructive weapon ever used. The atomic bomb produces a huge amount of blast, shock, heat, and deadly radiation. In August 1945, the United States dropped atomic bombs on the Japanese cities of Hiroshima and Nagasaki. More than 100,000 people died from the two bombings.

Wartime inventions brought some benefits. The **jet** engine that was first used in warplanes powered new and faster passenger planes in peacetime. And radar, an instrument used to detect and locate moving objects, was invented for military use. Today, it plays an important role in air travel and weather forecasting.

Did You Know?

No one knows who invented the gun. Evidence shows that handheld cannonlike weapons may have been used in China in the A.D. 1100's. The first guns were brass or iron tubes with a small hole at the closed end for setting fire to the gunpowder.

The thousands of inventions and discoveries brought about by social needs have eased health threats and helped people live longer. Many such discoveries have made our lives easier and more comfortable.

Through the microscope

Before the 1500's, doctors had little idea of what caused disease. Then about 1590, a Dutch spectacle-maker named Zacharias Janssen made the first compound microscope (an instrument that magnifies extremely small objects). Janssen's microscope had two or more sets of lenses to provide higher magnifications than the microscopes used previously. It used glass lenses, like those used for making eyeglasses, which had been available since the late 1200's.

In the mid-1670's, a Dutchman named Anton van Leeuwenhoek (*LAY vuhn hook*) used his microscope to study organisms (living things) invisible to the unaided eye. He discovered the microscopic organisms that are now called **bacteria.** Leeuwenhoek did not understand what these strange organisms were, but his studies led scientists to discover that certain bacteria and other germs cause disease.

Edward Jenner risked his reputation as a doctor when he gave the first vaccination for smallpox to a child in 1796.

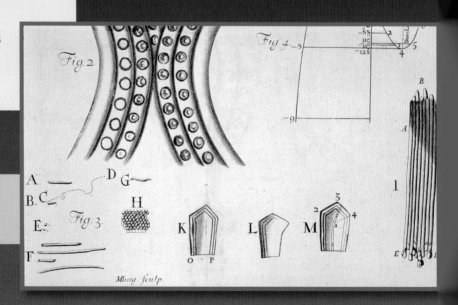

Anton van Leeuwenhoek drew illustrations of the bacteria he viewed under his microscope in the 1600's.

The first vaccine

In the 1700's, people dreaded catching the disease smallpox, which could kill or leave terrible scars on the body. However, some victims recovered from the disease and never caught smallpox again. They had developed lifelong **immunity** (resistance) to it. In 1796, an English doctor named Edward Jenner discovered a safe method of making people immune to smallpox.

Jenner and others had observed that dairymaids who caught cowpox—a relatively harmless disease that caused sores on the hands—did not catch smallpox. To test this theory, Jenner took matter from a dairymaid's cowpox sore and inserted it into a cut made on the arm of a healthy boy. The boy developed cowpox. But when Jenner later injected the boy with matter from a smallpox sore, the boy did not develop the disease. His body had built up an immunity to smallpox. Jenner had developed the first **vaccine.**

Inventions in the home

Look at the many appliances and products we now have in our homes to make life easier and more comfortable. Most have appeared since the late 1800's, when electric power became available. The vacuum cleaner, first manufactured around 1900, was just one of many devices that reduced housework. Refrigeration helped keep food fresh and brought convenience foods to the kitchen. Such electronic devices as calculators, televisions, and computers, are now taken for granted.

An Englishman named Hubert Cecil Booth invented one of the first vacuum cleaners in 1901. It was the size of a horse carriage and had to be pulled by horses from building to building. ▼

Early Inventions

From earliest times, people have been curious about the world around them. The first inventions appeared many thousands of years ago, during the Stone Age.

Stone Age inventors

The Old Stone Age lasted from about 2.5 million years ago to about 8000 B.C. During this time, people learned how to make axes and other tools by chipping bone, flint (a very hard mineral), horn, ivory, and stones into different shapes. They also invented the bow and arrow and the spear. These weapons helped early people hunt wild animals for food. Early people also discovered that they could make fire by striking flint against metal ore.

The first farmers

Later, people learned how to grow crops. They invented such tools as the hoe to grow better crops and to help in harvesting them. The development of agriculture meant that people no longer had to move from place to place in search of food. Early farmers began to settle in villages. From these villages grew the first cities. Over time, people developed new skills, such as making pottery and weaving cloth.

Cuneiform writing consists of wedge-shaped characters stamped on clay.

Stone Age people made such flint tools as arrow heads and spear heads (bottom left). Flint scrapers (below) were used on such materials as hides, wood, and bone.

Wheels, like many early tools, were sometimes made of stone.

Egyptian fishermen in a boat made of reeds pull a fish-laden net from the Nile River. The Nile was the lifeblood of ancient Egypt. Its floodwaters deposited rich, black soil on the land year after year, enabling farmers to grow huge grain crops. It also provided water for **irrigating** these crops in a hot, dry climate.

Metals and the wheel

No one knows when people first made objects from metal. As early as 3500 B.C., people had learned that tin and copper could be melted to make bronze. Bronze was stronger and lasted longer than either tin or copper.

About the same time, the wheel was invented. Before the invention of the wheel, people carried loads on their backs or dragged them on heavy sleds. The invention of the wheel led to the development of wagons, which enabled people to move goods more easily and over longer distances.

The first civilizations

The first **civilizations** (organized societies) developed between about 3500 and 3100 B.C. between the Tigris (*TY grihs*) and Euphrates (*yoo FRAY teez*) rivers of Mesopotamia and in the Nile Valley of Egypt. The rivers flooded each year, depositing large amounts of rich soil for farming in the valleys.

Perhaps the most important invention of the early civilizations was writing. The Sumerians, who lived in southern Mesopotamia, developed the first system of writing. Historians believe the Sumerians invented the system about 3500 B.C. The invention of writing meant that people no longer had to remember all knowledge. They could write down ideas and information.

Did You Know?

The ancient Egyptians developed a form of picture writing, called hieroglyphics. Hieroglyphics used picture symbols to represent ideas and sounds. The hieroglyphic writing was used mostly for religious inscriptions on temples and stone monuments. The Egyptians also recorded the words and deeds of royalty. They called their writing *the words of God.*

A great civilization developed in Greece by about the 500's B.C. The ancient Greeks are best known for their achievements in the arts, philosophy, and science. But they also produced many inventions. The most important Greek inventors included Ctesibius, Archimedes, and Hero.

Archimedes was one of the most notable mathematicians and inventors in ancient times.

Ctesibius

Ctesibius *(tee SIHB ee uhs)* lived during the 200's B.C. in Alexandria, Egypt, then a great center of Greek learning and culture. He built the first piston pump, which consisted of a cylinder with a plunger inside. As the plunger was moved up and down, it created pressure that could be used to pump water.

Archimedes

Archimedes (*AHR kuh MEE deez*) lived during the 200's B.C. in Syracuse, a Greek city in Sicily. He is most famous for his great mathematical discoveries, but he also produced many inventions. The best known of his inventions is the Archimedean screw, which was designed to raise water from a lower level to a higher one. It was used in ancient Egypt to drain and **irrigate** (bring water to) land in the Nile Valley.

The Archimedean screw consisted of a screw tightly fitted inside a cylinder that had two open ends. The lower end of the device was placed in the water. Attached to the screw at its upper end was either a handle or a device that turned the screw when people walked on it. The turning action lifted the water up along the threads of the screw and out the upper end.

The Archimedean screw was used as an irrigation device.

Hero

Hero lived during the first century A.D. in Alexandria. His most important invention was the screw press, a device for squeezing the juice from grapes to make wine and from olives to make olive oil. Earlier presses provided only limited pressure, and so they left much of the juice in the fruits. The screw press had a threaded shaft attached to the wood block that squeezed the fruits. By turning the shaft, greater pressure could be applied to the grapes and olives. As a result, Hero's screw press squeezed much more liquid from the fruits than earlier presses did.

Pumping Action

Pumping devices have been used for thousands of years as an important means of moving water. The ancient Egyptians used water wheels with buckets mounted on them to move water for irrigation. The buckets scooped water from wells and streams and deposited it in ditches that carried the water to fields.

Ancient Greece was the birthplace of Western **civilization** about 2,500 years ago. The magnificent achievements of the ancient Greeks in government, science, philosophy, and the arts still influence our lives.

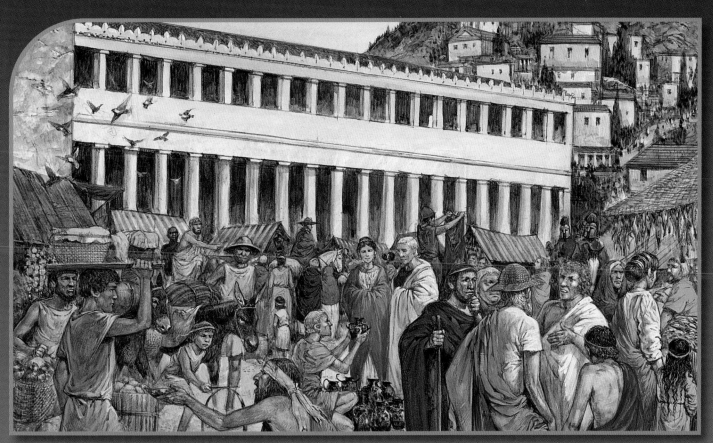

The Spread of Knowledge

Civilizations in Asia produced many advances in science and learning. As trade increased across the world, many of these inventions began to reach Europe.

Chinese inventions

More than 2,000 years ago, the Chinese invented paper. The Chinese also made the world's first porcelain, a type of ceramic valued for its beauty and strength.

Riding a horse became easier with the invention of the stirrup, which came from China to India and then to Europe in the A.D. 400's. The stirrup is a support for a rider's foot that hangs from the side of a saddle. It helped soldiers to fight on horseback with less risk of slipping off the horse.

The invention of the rigid horse collar made farming easier and helped overland travel. The rigid horse collar appeared in Europe about 800, but it was invented centuries earlier in China. Before this invention, horses wore a throat harness that cut off their breathing when they pulled too hard. The rigid collar shifted the pressure of the load to the horse's shoulders, enabling the animal to pull a much heavier load.

A porcelain vase and pedestal made in China in the 1200's. The Chinese made the first true porcelain—called China in the West—about 2,000 years ago.

An illustration from the 1400's shows European peasants performing a variety of farming tasks. The rigid collars around the necks of the horses allowed them to pull heavy loads, such as a plow turning the soil for planting.

Arab scholars

Scholars in the Arab world translated and preserved the works of ancient Greek mathematicians and made their own original contributions as well. A book written about 825 by the Arab mathematician al-Khwarizmi *(al KWAHR ihz mee)* described a numeration system developed in India. This decimal system used place values and zero. It became known as the Hindu-Arabic numeral system, which we still use today. Al-Khwarizmi also wrote an influential book about algebra, a branch of mathematics. The word *algebra* comes from the Arabic title of this book.

In the mid-1100's, a Latin translation of al-Khwarizmi's book on arithmetic introduced the Hindu-Arabic numeral system to Europe. In 1202, Leonardo Fibonacci, an Italian mathematician, published a book on algebra that helped promote this system. Hindu-Arabic numerals gradually replaced Roman numerals in Europe.

Arab scholars also contributed greatly to medicine. Rhazes, a Persian-born doctor of the late 800's and early 900's, wrote the first accurate descriptions of measles and smallpox. Avicenna, a Muslim (follower of the religion of Islam) doctor of the late 900's and early 1000's, produced a medical encyclopedia called *Canon of Medicine.* It summed up medical knowledge of the time and accurately described many diseases. The work became popular in Europe, where it influenced medical education for more than 600 years.

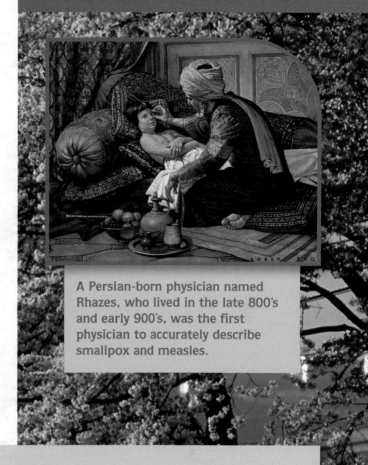

A Persian-born physician named Rhazes, who lived in the late 800's and early 900's, was the first physician to accurately describe smallpox and measles.

Wonders of China

Westerners who visited China in the 1200's were amazed at the wonders they saw. The Chinese people produced many of the world's most important inventions.

- The Chinese made glazed pottery some 2,000 years ago.

- The Chinese invented the wheelbarrow in the A.D. 300's. This simple but useful load-carrier did not appear in Europe until the 1200's.

- The Chinese were the first to make silk using silkworms. No one in the West saw the mysterious worm (actually a caterpillar) until about A.D. 550.

- Chinese ships were the first to use sternpost rudders. Before this invention, ships were steered by large, awkward oars that often broke during storms.

Inventions at Sea

Water transportation benefited from several inventions that spread during the Middle Ages—the period in European history between the A.D. 400's and 1400's. These inventions helped make possible the great voyages that led to the exploration of the New World.

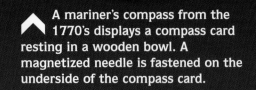

New sails

For several thousand years, square sails had been widely used, but they worked well only when the wind blew from behind a ship. Around A.D. 200, triangular sails called lateen sails appeared. Use of these sails spread during the Middle Ages. Lateen sails worked well when a ship sailed into the wind. Sailors mounted the two types of sails onto ships so they could sail in any condition.

▲ A mariner's compass from the 1770's displays a compass card resting in a wooden bowl. A magnetized needle is fastened on the underside of the compass card.

Easier navigation

Chinese sailors probably first used magnetic compasses to guide their ships in about the 1000's or 1100's. These compasses were simple pieces of magnetic iron, usually floated on straw or cork in a bowl of water. They used Earth's magnetic field to indicate direction.

The magnetic compass enabled sailors to **navigate** accurately when they could not see land and when they could not use the stars or sun as guides. It had reached Europe from China by 1200.

The carrack was a sailing vessel used in the 1400's and 1500's. Its square sails provided power when winds blew from behind. The triangular sails enabled the ship to sail into the wind.

Better steering

The sternpost rudder appeared about 1300. It consisted of a piece of wood or metal connected to a long upright post in the back of the boat. Prior to this invention, ships were steered by large oars near the stern, or rear of the ship. These steering oars were awkward and often broke during storms. The use of steering oars also limited the size of many ships and how far they could sail from land. The sternpost rudder could be used to steer larger ships. It also enabled the ships to sail safely in rough seas.

Did You Know?

In ancient times, sea travel was slow and difficult. Sailors lacked navigation instruments. As a result, they usually stayed within sight of land. The ships were hard to steer because they had no rudder. Sailors steered them by means of one or two oars at the stern. In addition, the ships could not depend entirely on the wind for power. The earliest ships had a single sail, which worked well only when the wind blew from behind. For times when there was no wind, many ships had teams of rowers.

Sternpost rudder

The sternpost rudder made it easier for people to steer large sailing ships.

The Age of Ideas

A time of new ideas and exploration flourished in Europe from about 1300 to 1600. This period is called the Renaissance *(REHN uh sahns)*—a Latin term meaning "rebirth." During the Renaissance, the study of medicine and other sciences, art, literature, and history gained new significance.

The printing press

About 1440, a German goldsmith named Johannes *(YOH HAHN UHS)* Gutenberg developed the modern printing press. The printing press used movable type, in which letters and other symbols are carved or stamped on individual plates. It was based on the design of the wine press, a machine that pressed the juice from grapes to make wine. Gutenberg assembled the pieces of metal type in a frame to form pages and applied ink to the type. The machine pressed the inked type against paper to print words.

Prior to the invention of printing, books were made by hand—a process that could take years. Most people could not read, and only clergyman and the upper class pursued learning. Within 10 years of Gutenberg's invention, people set up printing shops across Europe, especially in such major cities as London, Paris, and Venice. By 1500, millions of books had been printed. Gutenberg's invention put more knowledge into the hands of more people at less cost than ever before.

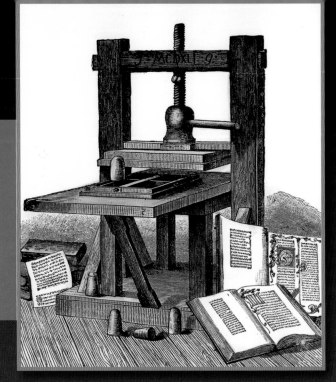

Gutenberg's printing press was adapted from a cheese or wine press and could print about 300 sheets a day.

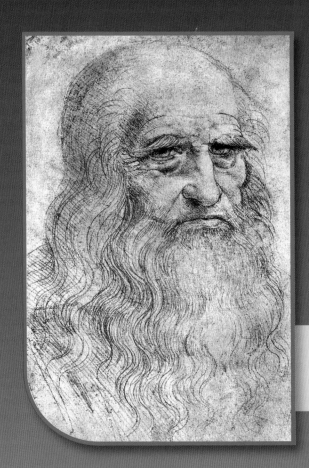

Bodies and blood

Before the Renaissance, people thought the study of religion was the most important branch of learning. Most societies had strictly limited the practice of dissecting (cutting up) human corpses for scientific study. But laws against dissection were relaxed during the Renaissance. As a result, the first truly scientific studies of the human body began.

In the 1500's, an Italian doctor and professor of medicine named Andreas Vesalius (*ahn DREH ahs vih SAY lee uhs*) examined dead bodies to learn more about how the human body worked. He wrote the first scientific textbook on human anatomy (structure) in 1543.

In the early 1600's, the English doctor William Harvey discovered how blood circulates through the body. He found that the heart pumps blood through the arteries to all parts of the body and that the blood returns to the heart through the veins. Harvey's work marked a turning point in medical history.

Leonardo da Vinci

Leonardo da Vinci (1452-1519) was one of the key figures of the Renaissance and one of the most versatile geniuses in history. He became one of the world's greatest painters, but he also studied the human body, **astronomy,** plants, and rocks. He designed machines and drew plans for hundreds of inventions. Many of his ideas, such as his plans for a flying machine, were far ahead of his time.

Leonardo da Vinci's self-portrait was drawn when he was about 60 years old. It is the only existing likeness of the artist.

Leonardo's Notebooks

Leonardo da Vinci recorded his ideas in notebooks. About 4,200 pages of these notebooks still exist. They include sketches of machines and the first accurate drawings of the human body. Leonardo wrote his notes backward, so they can be read only if the page is held up to a mirror.

Human muscles are shown in an illustration from Andreas Vesalius's *On the Structure of the Human Body, or Fabrica* (1543). This was the first scientific text on human anatomy.

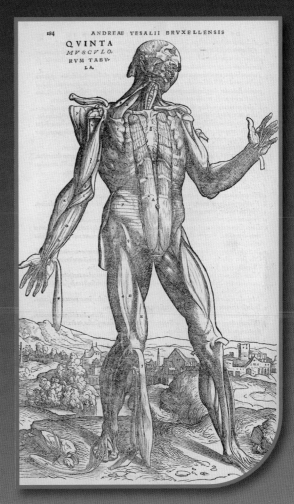

From the earliest times, people have searched the sky for explanations, clues to our own existence, and answers to the mysteries of the natural world. During the Renaissance, scholars made new discoveries in astronomy and challenged ideas that had been held for centuries.

The system of the universe proposed by Copernicus in 1543 placed the sun, not Earth, at the center.

The sun and the planets

Before the 1500's, **astronomers** believed Earth was the center of the universe and stayed motionless. Then in 1543, the Polish astronomer Nicolaus Copernicus put forward a new theory. He claimed that Earth and the other planets revolve around the sun.

Other astronomers built on Copernicus's work. In the late 1500's, the Danish astronomer Tycho Brahe *(TEE koh brah)* observed the movement of the planets far more precisely than ever before. Then Brahe's assistant, Johannes Kepler of Germany, discovered that the planets travel around the sun in an oval-shaped path, or ellipse. Copernicus had thought that the planets moved around the sun in circles.

Johannes Kepler (left) and Tycho Brahe studied the underlying principles of planetary motion.

1600's helped astronomers observe the sky in greater detail. A telescope is an instrument with lenses and a tube. It is used to make distant objects seem closer and larger. The telescope was probably first made by a Dutch optician named Hans Lippershey in 1608, when he mounted two glass lenses inside a narrow tube. News of the invention spread quickly.

Within a year, the Italian astronomer Galileo *(GAL uh LAY oh)* had made his own telescope and turned it to the stars. There he saw four moons revolving around the planet Jupiter. At the time, most people still believed that the stars, planets, and moons revolved around Earth. He proved that this was untrue. The invention of the telescope helped prove that Copernicus had been right about the motion of the planets.

Galileo also looked at the moon through his telescope. He discovered that, far from being perfectly smooth as the ancient Greeks had thought, the moon had a rough surface with mountains and craters.

Telescopes built by the Italian astronomer Galileo were larger and more powerful than the telescopes that had been made previously.

The Power of the Church

The idea that Earth revolves around the sun went against church teachings of the time. Between about the 1100's and 1500's, the Roman Catholic Church punished people who spoke in favor of such ideas. Galileo, who supported Copernicus's theory of planetary motion, was sentenced to life imprisonment under house arrest in 1633. He was also forced to say that such ideas were untrue. The Roman Catholic Church finally absolved (declared free from guilt) Galileo in 1992.

a New World

By the 1600's, new discoveries by scientists rapidly increased scientific knowledge. One of the most notable scientists of the time was Isaac Newton.

The young scientist

Isaac Newton was born in Lincolnshire, England, in 1642. As a boy, he enjoyed making machines more than studying. He invented a small windmill for grinding wheat and two objects for measuring time—a water clock and a sundial. As a young man, Newton became a student at Cambridge University, though he showed no particular promise. However, between 1665 and 1667, Newton made discoveries that changed the way we see the world.

What stops the universe from falling apart?

Newton left Cambridge during an outbreak of plague (a deadly disease) and went to live in the country. During this time, he made an important discovery about gravitation—the natural force that draws the objects of the universe toward each other.

When Newton was 23, the sight of an apple falling from a tree caused him to question how far the force of gravity reaches. He realized that the same force that pulled the apple from the tree holds the moon in its orbit (path) around Earth. Likewise, the gravitational force of the sun keeps the planets in their orbits. Newton also proved that many types of motion are due to the force of gravity.

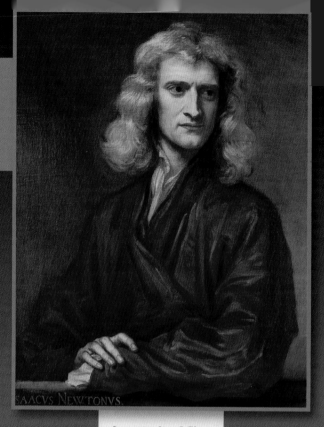

ISAACVS NEWTONVS.

A portrait of Sir Isaac Newton painted in 1689 by Sir Godfrey Kneller. The portrait was made two years after Newton published his theory of gravitation.

Facts About Newton

- Isaac Newton was born on Christmas Day in 1642, the same year that the Italian astronomer Galileo died.

- Newton left school when he was 14 to help his widowed mother with her farm. But he spent so much time reading, he was sent back to school.

- Newton was so sensitive to criticism of his scientific theories that his friends had to plead with him to publish his most valuable discoveries.

- Despite his great achievements, Newton modestly described himself as "like a boy playing on the seashore, and diverting myself in now and then finding a smoother pebble or a prettier shell than ordinary, while the great ocean of truth lay all undiscovered before me."

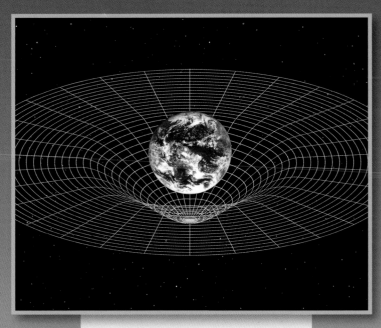

Newton discovered how the universe is held together by gravity. The gravitational pull of a large object weakens over a distance.

Newton's other discoveries

Newton made many other important contributions to science. He discovered the properties of light and color. And he helped to establish a branch of mathematics called calculus, which deals with finding areas of curved shapes.

The world hears of Newton's work

Although Newton finished his first investigations on gravity and motion by 1666, nothing more was heard of them for nearly 20 years. Meanwhile, Newton continued to teach mathematics at Cambridge, where he was a professor.

At a meeting of scientists in 1684, **astronomer** Edmond Halley, scientist Robert Hooke, and architect Christopher Wren were discussing the force that makes the planets move around the sun. What is it? The three men could not solve this problem. Halley went to see Newton. He found that the Cambridge professor had a complete proof of the law of gravity.

Halley persuaded Newton to publish his findings, and they appeared in 1687 in *Philosophiae Naturalis Principia Mathematica (Mathematical Principles of Natural Philosophy)*. This book was the first to present a unified system of scientific principles explaining what happens on Earth and in the heavens. Modern physics, a branch of science that deals with matter and energy, would not have been possible without Newton's discoveries.

The Industrial Revolution

The 1700's and early 1800's were times of rapid change for the people of Europe and North America. The development of large industries (businesses) and the invention of new machines greatly affected people's way of life and the type of work they did. This period of change began in Great Britain. It is known as the Industrial Revolution.

Thomas Newcomen's steam engine drove a pump to remove water from mines. The machine was bulky and wasted fuel. It turned only a fraction of the energy it received into useful work.

Steam for pumps

The driving force of industrialization was the **steam engine,** a machine operated by the energy of expanding steam. An Englishman named Thomas Savery designed the first practical steam engine in 1698. It was used as a pump to drain water from mines—areas where natural resources are dug out of the earth from open pits. The English inventor Thomas Newcomen built the first commercial steam engine in 1712.

Watt's engines

In the 1760's and 1770's, the Scottish **engineer** James Watt worked to improve the steam engine. Watt's engines used steam and fuel more efficiently than early steam engines. They also could do a variety of tasks other than pumping. A linking mechanism changed the up-and-down motion of the engine into rotary, or round-and-round, motion. The improved Watt engines could now drive other machines.

By the early 1800's, other inventors had built engines that used steam at high pressure. These engines produced even greater power.

In textile mills, women operated looms powered by steam engines or water wheels.

Machines and factories

The introduction of power-driven machinery and the development of factory organization created an enormous increase in the production of goods. Before the **Industrial Revolution,** manufacturing was done by hand or by using animal power or simple machines. During the revolution, power-driven machines replaced handwork, and factories developed as the most economical way of bringing together the machines and the workers to operate them.

Textile machines

In the 1760's, two machines revolution-ized the textile (woven fabric) industry: the spinning jenny and the water frame. The English weaver James Hargreaves invented the spinning jenny in 1764. The machine could spin more than one yarn at a time. In 1769, another Englishman, Richard Arkwright, invented the water frame. It was a type of spinning machine powered by water.

In the 1770's, a British weaver named Samuel Crompton invented the spinning mule, a machine that combined features of the spinning jenny and the water frame. The spinning mule ended the home-spinning industry. However, weaving was still done on handlooms until the mid-1780's, when an English-man named Edmund Cartwright developed a steam-powered loom. Soon weaving, too, became a factory process.

Large ironworks made the United Kingdom the world's leading iron producer during the Industrial Revolution.

Steam on Water, Steam on Rails

The invention of the steam engine started the greatest revolution in transportation since the invention of the wheel and the sailing ship.

Fulton's steamboat

The American steamboat pioneer Robert Fulton was born on a farm in Pennsylvania in 1765. As a boy, he made household utensils for his mother and fireworks for a town celebration. He became a painter and went to England to study art, but he was more interested in inventing. He designed canal boats and a machine for digging canals (manmade waterways).

In 1801, Fulton built a submarine called the *Nautilus*, which was able to dive and surface. His ideas about underwater craft interested both the French and British governments, but neither adopted them wholeheartedly. In 1803, Fulton learned that a steam-powered boat had been tested on the Seine River in Paris. Fulton ordered one of James Watt's **steam engines** and returned to the United States, where he constructed his own steamboat.

The *Clermont*, built by Robert Fulton, was the first steamboat to carry paying passengers. Its first successful voyage was a trip up the Hudson River.

Up the river

Fulton's craft was registered as the *North River Steamboat of Clermont,* but it was generally called the *Clermont.* It traveled from New York City to Albany in 1807, and soon it was providing regular passenger service on the Hudson River. In 1819, the American ship *Savannah* became the first steam-powered vessel to cross the Atlantic Ocean. However, it used sails for most of the 29-day trip.

Pulling power

In 1801, the British **engineer** Richard Trevithick built a steam carriage that ran on the road. In 1804, he built the first steam **locomotive** to run on rails. A locomotive is a machine that moves trains on railroad tracks. Trevithick's locomotive pulled a load of iron along a railroad made for horse-drawn trucks.

In 1829, the British engineer Robert Stephenson designed and built the *Rocket,* the first steam locomotive suitable for high-speed, long-distance use. That year, a company in New York imported four British locomotives for use in Pennsylvania. One of these, the *Stourbridge Lion,* became the first locomotive to operate on a commercial railroad in the United States.

Steam railroads

The first steam railroad to run regular freight services began in the United Kingdom in 1825, and a passenger railroad opened in 1830. The locomotives hauling the trains were built by George Stephenson, a British engineer.

Steamboat Firsts

- In 1783, the Marquis Claude de Jouffroy d'Abbans, a French nobleman, built a steamboat that made a 15-minute river trip.

- In 1787, John Fitch, an American inventor, made the first workable steamboat in the United States. Its engine powered a series of paddles on each side of the boat. Fitch started a passenger service in 1790, but lacked the money to keep operating.

- In 1802, William Symington, a British engineer, built a steam tug that had a paddlewheel at the stern. It worked perfectly, but Symington also ran out of money.

- In 1809, the *Phoenix* became the first steamboat to make an ocean voyage as it chugged from New York City to Philadelphia. This steamboat was built by John Stevens, an American engineer.

- In 1838, the British steamer *Sirius* became the first ship to offer regular scheduled service across the Atlantic Ocean under steam power alone.

Railroads began carrying freight and passengers in the 1830's. On some railroads, horses as well as steam locomotives were used to pull wagons. Steam locomotives could pull heavier trains faster than horses.

Before the invention of powered machines, people used horses, mules, and oxen to work their fields, or they worked with their hands. New machines changed farm life in the 1800's.

The first successful harvesting machine, the reaper, was invented by Cyrus McCormick in 1831.

McCormick's reaper

Cyrus McCormick was born in 1809 on a farm in Virginia. He experimented with machinery to make farming easier. At harvest time, farmers still cut their crops with hand scythes *(syths)*—cutting tools that had changed little in thousands of years.

In 1831, Cyrus built his first reaper. This machine had a straight cutting blade linked by gears to a drive wheel. As the wheel turned, the blade moved back and forth and sawed through the stalks of grain. Projecting rods caught and held the stalks while the blade cut through them. The stalks fell onto a platform, where a worker raked them onto the ground. Several other workers bound the bundles of grain. The machine sold well, and McCormick gained worldwide fame.

Later inventors worked to improve the reaper so that fewer workers were needed. In the 1870's, the American inventor Sylvanus D. Locke produced a binder that bound the sheaves (bundles of grain) and dropped them on the ground.

Today, reapers have been replaced by combined harvester-threshers, or combines. These machines cut the stalks and separate the seeds from them as they move across a field.

An early threshing machine was powered by horses walking on a treadmill. Threshing removed grain from the stalks of cereal crops.

Steam-driven traction engines pulled and powered farm equipment.

The tractor

In 1870's, the first steam-powered tractors appeared. They were strong enough to pull 40 plows at once, but they hardly moved. In fact, most did not move at all. They were simply traction (pulling) engines. They could pull objects, but they could not push them.

By the late 1800's, **engineers** had developed the gasoline engine for use in automobiles. In 1892, an Iowa farmer named John Froelich used this technology to build the first practical gasoline-powered tractor. Unlike earlier tractors, Froelich's tractor could move forward and backward. Froelich attached his tractor to a threshing machine for separating kernels of grains from stalks.

The Plow

About 8,000 years ago, unknown farmers sharpened one prong of a forked branch to turn the soil. The plow had been invented. Today, there are four chief kinds of plows:

- The tractor plow is pulled by a tractor. It has furrowing spades mounted on its frame.

- The walking plow is pulled by oxen, horses, or mules. The farmer walks behind to steer the plow.

- The sulky plow has a seat and wheels, so the farmer can ride while preparing the soil. It was invented in 1875 by John Deere, an Illinois blacksmith. Horses pull the sulky plow.

- The gang plow, a horse- or tractor-drawn plow, also allows the farmer to ride while tilling. It has two or more bottoms and three wheels. A gang plow can till as many paths at a time as it has bottoms.

Today, we would find it hard to live, work, or play without electric power. Electric power makes many household machines work at the flick of a switch.

Electricity in nature

People knew about electricity as early as the 500's B.C. They observed that amber—a hard, fossilized substance from pine trees that grew millions of years ago—attracted small pieces of straw after being rubbed with cloth. This force of attraction is called static electricity. You can generate static electricity by combing your hair briskly on a dry day.

Edison's screw-in lightbulb was the first light bulb to be produced on a large scale.

Electric lights lit up London as early as the 1880's.

Lights On!

For thousands of years, people relied on oil lamps and candles to give light at night. During the 1800's, gas lamps and kerosene lamps brought light to homes and streets.

In the mid-1800's, inventors tried to create light from electricity using battery powered lamps. However, the widespread use of electric light required not only a lamp, but also a cheap method of distributing electric power to homes and businesses. The American inventor Thomas Edison developed such a method. His first power plant for generating and distributing electric power began to operate in 1882 in New York City.

Michael Faraday discovered the principal of **electromagnetic** induction, which led to the development of the electric motor.

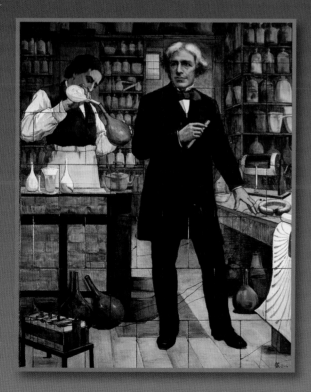

Experiments with electric charge

In 1786, an Italian professor named Luigi Galvani made a discovery that would lead to the development of batteries—devices that convert chemical energy into electric energy. Galvani hung a dead frog by the legs to a copper hook and hung the hook over an iron railing. The frog's legs twitched when they touched the railing. Galvani thought, wrongly, that the legs contained "animal electricity."

In the late 1790's, the Italian scientist Alessandro Volta discovered what made the frog's legs twitch. The chemical action of moisture and two metals, such as the iron and copper in Galvani's experiment, produced electricity. Volta then built the first battery and produced the first source of steady electric current.

Electricity and magnetism

In 1831, Michael Faraday of England and Joseph Henry of the United States independently made a discovery that led to the development of electric power as an important source of energy. Faraday and Henry found that moving a magnet through a coil of copper wire caused an electric current to flow in the wire. This discovery led to the development of the electric motor—a machine that changes electric power into mechanical power. By the 1840's, electric motors were operating such machines as **telegraphs.** By 1900, electric vehicles and home appliances were powered by such motors.

Experiments with electricity and magnetism also led to the development of the electric generator—a machine that changes mechanical energy into electrical energy. Today, electric generators produce almost all the electric power used by people. They furnish electric power that runs machines in factories, provides lighting, and operates home appliances.

The 1800's brought advancements in printing methods, allowing news and information to spread more rapidly. But high-speed communication truly began with the invention of the telegraph and the telephone.

Printing picks up steam

In 1811, the German printer Friedrich Konig became the first person to use a **steam engine** to power a press. Although printers continued to set type by hand, they could now print materials hundreds of times faster, and so could produce large numbers of copies cheaply. By the mid-1800's, wide access to printed materials had led to a rapid increase in literacy in industrialized countries.

The telegraph

Steamships and **locomotives** increased the speed at which people and news could travel. But high-speed communication truly began with the electric **telegraph,** a device that sent messages by using electric current traveling along wires. The first successful telegraph system was developed by the American painter and inventor Samuel F. B. Morse and his partner, Alfred Vail. Telegraph messages were sent in a code of dots and dashes known as Morse code.

The telegraph rapidly became the chief means of fast long-distance communication. Newspapers began to use the Morse telegraph at once. By the 1860's, telegraph lines linked most major U.S. cities. A telegraph cable was laid across the floor of the Atlantic Ocean in 1866.

The telegraph was an important means of communication from the mid-1800's to the mid-1900's.

Konig's steam-powered printing press could only print one side of a sheet at a time. However, it could print 1,100 sheets an hour, making it far more efficient than any previous printing press.

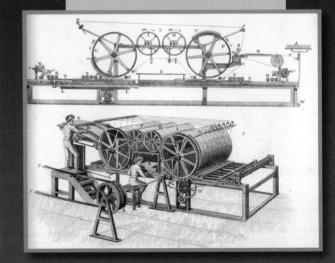

Calling Mr. Watson

In 1871, a Scot named Alexander Graham Bell immigrated to the United States. He worked as a teacher of the deaf in Boston, and in his spare time he experimented with a device for sending several telegraph messages at once over one wire. On June 2, 1875, one of the metal reeds in this device stuck. Bell's assistant, Thomas A. Watson, plucked the reed to loosen it. Bell was in another room but heard the vibration in his receiver. He realized that the vibrating reed had caused variations of electric current. In turn, the electric current had reproduced the same variations in the receiver he was using.

On March 10, 1876, Bell was testing a new **transmitter,** the part of the telegraph that converts sound waves into electrical signals and sends them to a receiver. As Bell did so, Watson waited in another room for the test message. Suddenly, Bell spilled some acid from a battery on his clothes. He cried out: "Mr. Watson, come here. I want you!" Watson heard every word and rushed into the room. Bell had invented the telephone.

Telephone services soon began operating in the United States and other parts of the world.

Alexander Graham Bell demonstrates the usefulness of the telephone to businessmen in 1892 by placing a call to Chicago from New York City. ❯

Did You Know?

In 1891, the first international telephone connection was established between London and Paris. In 1892, phone service began between New York City and Chicago. Telephone service reached all major urban centers across the world by 1950.

Capturing Images and Motion

The saying "a picture is worth a thousand words" expresses the power of images. Photographs and motion pictures enhance our understanding of people and places in the world, as well as historical events. Their development created new forms of artistic expression.

Early photographs

Many American, British, and French scientists contributed to the development of photography, and no one person can be called its inventor. In 1826, a French scientist named Joseph Nicéphore Niépce (*zhoh ZEHF nee say FAWR nyehps*) made the first permanent photograph. Niépce's technique involved exposing a chemically coated metal plate to an image for about eight hours. The chemical absorbed only the light areas of the image and washed away where the areas were dark. The plate had made a direct, positive copy of the image.

The French painter Louis J. M. Daguerre worked as Niépce's partner for several years. In the 1830's, Daguerre developed the daguerreotype *(duh GEHR uh typ)*, a type of photograph that took only a few minutes to expose. At about the same time, the British inventor William Henry Fox Talbot devised a photographic method that used a paper negative. Fox Talbot's invention was not widely used because it produced less clear pictures than a daguerreotype. But the idea of using a flexible negative became the key to modern photography. The glass or metal plates used in other methods had to be changed after each exposure. With Fox Talbot's method, film could be moved through the camera and used to take a series of pictures.

George Eastman (above) made photography more accessible when he introduced the Kodak camera in 1888. The Kodak contained film wound on rollers, eliminating the need for glass photographic plates.

The daguerreotype, popular during the 1840's and 1850's, was the first practical, popular method of photography. The image was made on a sheet of silver-coated copper, developed with heated mercury fumes, and then "fixed" with table salt.

Advances in film

In 1887, an American clergyman named Hannibal W. Goodwin developed a strip of film made of celluloid, a tough but flexible material. George Eastman, who made photographic equipment, introduced the film in 1889. This launched the age of the personal camera and the snapshot.

Motion pictures

The first successful photographs of motion were made in 1877 and 1878 by Eadweard Muybridge (*EHD wurd MY brihj*), a British photographer working in California. Muybridge took a series of photographs of a running horse. For his project, Muybridge set up a row of cameras (first 12, then 24) with strings attached to their shutters. When the horse ran by, it broke each string in succession, tripping the shutters.

Muybridge's feat influenced inventors in several countries to work toward developing devices to record and represent moving images. Through their efforts, several different types of motion-picture cameras and projectors appeared in the mid-1890's.

The birth of the cinema

Film screenings soon became a popular entertainment. In large cities, motion pictures played on vaudeville programs, in music halls, and in amusement arcades. Traveling projectionists brought the films to smaller cities and country towns. The most popular subjects included re-creations of current news events, such as battles in the Spanish-American War of 1898, and dramatized folk tales.

Lights, Cameras, Action!

A camera works in much the same way as the human eye. However, there are special cameras that can "see" events in a way that the eye cannot. Such cameras capture images in deep space, at the bottom of the ocean, and inside the human body. Cameras also help in battling crime and fighting wars. Hidden cameras can take pictures that help the police find criminals. Aerial photographs help military leaders learn about the movement of enemy troops.

Eadweard Muybridge used a row of cameras to capture the motion of a running horse.

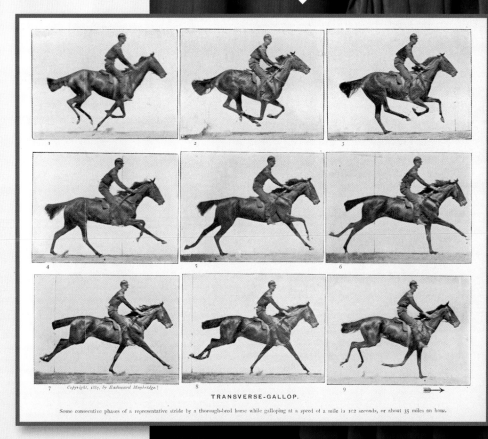

1   2   3   4   5   6   7   8   9

Copyright, 1887, by Eadweard Muybridge.

TRANSVERSE-GALLOP.

Some consecutive phases of a representative stride by a thorough-bred horse while galloping at a speed of a mile in 102 seconds, or about 35 miles an hour.

The Great Inventor

Thomas Edison was one of the greatest inventors in history and an important industrial leader. Edison loved making inventions and wanted them to benefit many people.

The young inventor

Thomas Alva Edison (1847-1931) was mainly educated by his mother, a former teacher. As a boy, he read science books and made working models of a sawmill and a steam railroad **locomotive.** He also had an eye for business, growing vegetables on the family farm and selling them in town.

At age 12, Edison began to sell newspapers and sandwiches on passenger trains between his hometown of Port Huron, Michigan, and Detroit. He used the baggage car of the train as a laboratory to do chemical experiments. By the time he was 15, Edison was publishing and selling his own newspaper.

Telegraph innovator

In 1863, Edison started work as a **telegraph** operator. Despite increasing difficulty with his hearing, he mastered the art of receiving news reports by telegraph. He also made improvements to the telegraph equipment.

While working in New York City in 1869, Edison improved the stock tickers—machines that recorded stock transactions on a 1-inch (2.5-centimeter) wide paper called ticker tape. He set up a company to make stock tickers, and was joined by other mechanically talented associates.

Thomas Edison was one of the greatest inventors and industrial leaders in history.

Edison's team invented the kinetoscope, the first device to show motion pictures. Kinetoscope parlors first opened in New York and London in 1894, but their popularity faded after the introduction of cinema the next year. ▼

south of Newark, New Jersey. He tinkered with the "speaking telegraph," as the newly invented telephone was called. He also invented the phonograph, a machine for recording and playing back sounds. Edison himself made the first recording—of "Mary Had a Little Lamb"—in 1877. The phonograph made Edison famous as the "Wizard of Menlo Park."

Edison then began to work on electric lighting. By 1879, he and his researchers had successfully tested an incandescent light bulb. This type of light bulb uses an electric current to heat a coil of wire inside a glass bulb. The coil of wire gives off light when the electric current passes through it.

Electric light was a novelty at first because few homes and businesses had electric power. Edison began experimenting to produce electric power cheaply. By the 1890's, hundreds of communities throughout the world had Edison power stations.

Work with motion pictures

In 1886, Edison moved to a much larger laboratory, where there was space for chemical, mechanical, and electrical experiments. A meeting with British-born photographer Eadweard Muybridge inspired Edison to investigate moving pictures recorded on film. He and his research team invented the kinetoscope *(kih NEHT uh skohp),* a coin-operated machine that showed a short movie through a peephole or eyepiece. They made a motion-picture camera and projector, and set up the first film studio.

Edison continued to make inventions throughout his life. He obtained 1,093 United States **patents**—government grants that give a person exclusive rights to an invention for a limited time. Edison believed in working long and hard. He said, "Genius is 1 percent inspiration and 99 percent perspiration."

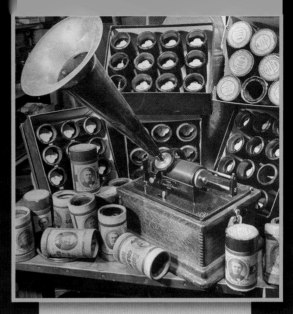

The phonograph recorded sound on a metal cylinder wrapped in tinfoil and then played back the sound.

Did You Know?

Edison's phonograph was so unusual that at first no one knew what to do with it. Edison thought it would be useful as a dictating machine. He also used it in toys, such as talking dolls and children's pianos. People later had the idea of selling musical recordings for the phonograph, and Edison began to make his own recordings.

People on Wheels

The automobile was invented in the 1880's. The development of the gasoline engine made this modern means of transportation possible. Cars, trucks, and buses soon crowded onto roads.

The gasoline engine

Several inventors in the 1800's tried to develop an engine that worked better than the **steam engine.** Jean Joseph Étienne Lenoir, a Belgian-born inventor living in France, built one of the first practical internal-combustion engines in 1860. Internal-combustion engines are powered by burning fuel inside a closed cylinder.

The internal-combustion engine was simpler, smaller, and more efficient than the steam engine, which burned fuel outside the cylinder. Lenoir's engine burned coke oven gas. It was used to drive machinery, though Lenoir also tried it in a motorcar. Other inventors also took up the challenge.

The first automobiles

In the 1880's, German **engineers** Gottlieb Daimler and Karl Benz separately developed vehicles driven by gasoline engines. Daimler and his partner Wilhelm Maybach made a motor bicycle in 1885 and a four-wheeled car in 1886. Karl Benz drove his first three-wheeled car in 1885. It had several features still common in cars today.

About 1891, William Morrison, an American inventor, built a successful electric car. Electric cars quickly became popular because they were quiet, easy to operate, emission-free, and reliable. But most electric cars could travel no faster than 20 miles (32 kilometers) per hour. The batteries had to be recharged at least every 50 miles (80 kilometers). By 1905, only a few of the cars sold were electrics.

Henry Ford revolutionized the young automobile industry by developing the assembly line method of production, which reduced the costs of manufacturing automobiles.

Car Firsts

- In 1885, Gottlieb Daimler and Karl Benz developed the first practical internal-combustion engine.

- In 1895, a French rubber-making firm, Michelin, introduced the first automobile tires filled with compressed air.

- In 1896, Henry Ford built his first successful car.

- In 1997, Toyota introduces the Prius, the first mass-produced hybrid car (an electric car that also has a combustion engine).

The electric self-starter

The automobile became a major means of transportation in the early 1900's, partly because of new inventions that made cars easier and safer to operate. In 1911, Charles F. Kettering, an American inventor, developed the electric self-starter for gasoline engines. Before the self-starter, auto engines were cranked by hand to be started. Hand-cranking was difficult, troublesome, and sometimes dangerous. Kettering's invention enabled a person to start an engine by simply pushing a button.

Mass production

Before 1900, skilled craftworkers made cars one at a time. However, **mass-production** methods had been used since the mid-1800's to produce firearms and farm equipment. To build vehicles faster, Henry Ford applied the same methods to carmaking.

In 1901 in the United States, Ransom E. Olds began to mass produce cars from parts sent in to his factory by outside suppliers. In 1913, Henry Ford installed a moving assembly line in his car factory. The frame of a car was pulled through the plant by a chain. Workers stood on each side and assembled the car by adding parts brought to them on moving conveyor belts. This system saved time and money.

Henry Ford sits in one of his Model T cars, which the company introduced in 1908. This simple and inexpensive automobile outsold all other cars for almost 20 years.

A replica of the Daimler Einspur shows what the first vehicle to use an internal combustion engine may have looked like. The vehicle reached a top speed of 7 miles (11.3 kilometers) per hour. >

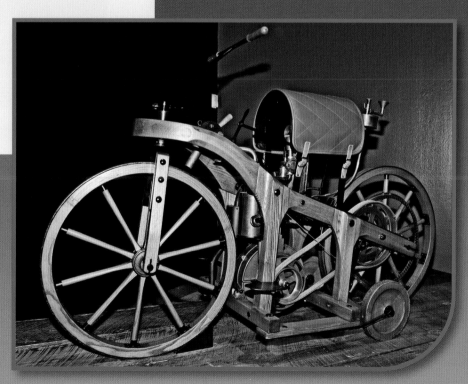

Medical Progress

Since the mid-1800's, discoveries in the field of medical science have brought new understanding about the causes of disease, as well as safer and more effective forms of treatment.

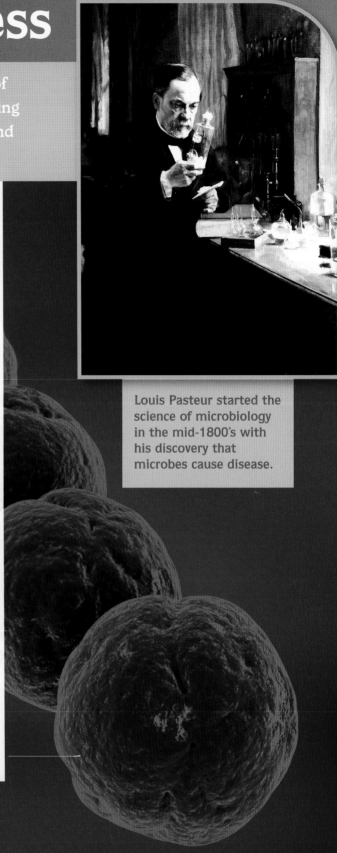

Louis Pasteur started the science of microbiology in the mid-1800's with his discovery that microbes cause disease.

Germs and disease

Scientists of the 1800's made dramatic progress in learning the causes of infectious disease. In the late 1800's, the French scientist Louis Pasteur proved that germs are living things and that some germs, such as certain **bacteria,** can cause disease. He also discovered that germs can be killed with heat.

Pasteur weakened germs in a laboratory so that they were less harmful. He then placed them in animals' bodies. These animals developed an **immunity** to the particular germ without becoming ill. Pasteur called this method of fighting off microbes **vaccination**.

The first anesthetic

For thousands of years, doctors tried to dull pain during surgery by administering alcoholic drinks, opium, and various other drugs. But no drug had proved effective in reducing the pain and shock of operations. Then in the 1840's, two Americans—Crawford Long and William T. G. Morton—separately discovered that ether *(EE thuhr)* gas could safely put patients to sleep during surgery. With this **anesthetic,** doctors could perform many operations that they could not attempt on conscious patients.

Safer surgery

Before the mid-1800's, hospitals were dirty and surgeons often operated wearing their street clothes. As a result, up to half of all surgical patients died of infections. Pasteur's early work on bacteria convinced the British surgeon Joseph Lister that germs caused many of these deaths. Lister used carbolic acid, a substance that destroys germs, to clean surgical wounds. Later doctors used a technique that involved keeping hospitals as clean as possible. Surgeons sterilized instruments and washed thoroughly before operating. They also wore surgical gowns, gloves, and masks.

The X ray

In 1895, the German scientist Wilhelm Roentgen *(REHNT guhn)* made an unexpected discovery while conducting an experiment. He had removed all the air from a glass tube and covered it with black paper. Then he ran an electric current through the tube. Afterward, he noticed that a dark image appeared on a photographic plate near the tube. Roentgen assumed that unknown, invisible rays, which he called X rays, were coming from the tube. These rays passed easily through some substances, such as flesh, but were largely stopped by others, such as metal or bone. Because of this, Roentgen found he could photograph the bone structure of his wife's hand with the rays.

X rays became the first of many technologies that enable doctors to "see" inside the human body to diagnose illnesses and injuries. In the late 1900's, scientists developed new imaging techniques that produce amazingly detailed views of internal body structures.

Did You Know?

The oldest-known surgical treatment was trephining. This operation was performed in the Stone Age, when a stone instrument was used to cut a hole into a person's skull. Scientists have found fossils of such skulls that are 10,000 years old. The operation was probably performed to release evil spirits believed to be causing headaches, mental illness, or epilepsy.

An early X-ray photograph by Wilhelm Roentgen shows his wife's left hand and wedding ring. Roentgen's discovery of X rays in 1895 caused a sensation. Within a few months, doctors were using X rays to examine broken bones.

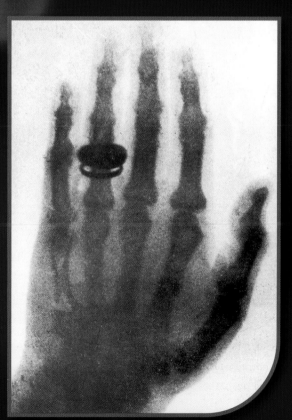

Advances in many fields of science and engineering created a medical revolution that lasted through the 1900's. Today, medical advances continue to change the way we treat and diagnose disease and other health problems.

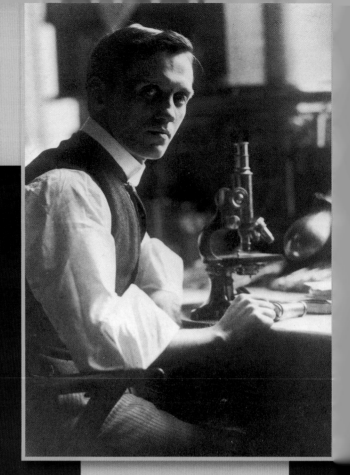

Penicillin

Today, penicillin is one of many antibiotics—drugs that destroy or weaken disease-causing germs. Its accidental discovery led to an entirely new way of treating infections and other illnesses.

In 1928, the English scientist Sir Alexander Fleming noticed mold growing in a lab dish containing common **bacteria.** The mold, called *Penicillium*, had killed the bacteria around it. In the 1930's, British researchers led by Howard Florey and Ernst Chain found a way to extract (pull out) and purify small amounts of penicillin. Penicillin became the first antibiotic. Scientists have since developed hundreds of antibiotics.

Discovery of genes

Since the 1980's, scientists have made significant progress in understanding genes—the tiny parts of cells that determine which characteristics living things inherit from their parents. Researchers successfully identified the genetic defects involved in some diseases. Doctors are hopeful that understanding genes will lead to new ways to treat or prevent disease.

Sir Alexander Fleming discovered the germ-killing power of the green mold, *Penicillium notatum*, in 1928. For his discovery, he shared the 1945 Nobel Prize in medicine with fellow British scientists Howard Florey and Ernst B. Chain. Florey and Chain helped develop the life-saving antibiotic, penicillin, from *Penicillium notatum*.

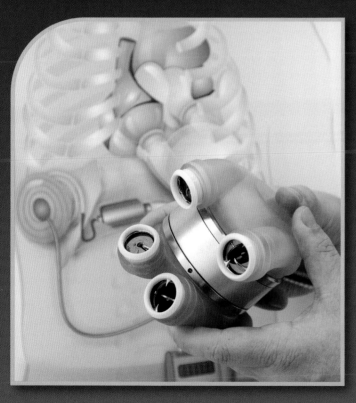

Stem cell research

Stem cells are cells that have the ability to develop into any of the different cell types that make up the tissues and organs of the body. Stem cells have the ability to divide endlessly, producing more stem cells or other types of cells.

In 1998, scientists isolated and grew the first stem cells from a human embryo. An embryo is an animal in an early stage of growth, before it has been born. Scientists think that stem cells can be used to replace damaged tissues and treat diseases. They may also be grown to form entire organs for transplants.

Scientists hope that stem cell research may lead to breakthroughs in the medical treatment for many diseases.

Medical engineering

Much progress in modern medicine has resulted from **engineering** advances. Engineers have developed a variety of instruments and devices to aid doctors in the diagnosis, treatment, and prevention of diseases. In many cases, doctors can now perform surgery through tiny incisions using small precision instruments. This technique reduces the trauma of surgery and shortens or avoids hospitalization. Engineers have also made great progress in creating highly advanced replacements for worn or damaged body parts. These replacements include artificial limbs, joints, and heart valves.

Scientists are working to refine and improve the design and function of artificial hearts so that the devices may eventually be used to permanently replace a diseased human heart.

The development of radio in the late 1800's revolutionized communication. Radio enabled people to communicate quickly between any two points on land, at sea, and—later—in the sky, and even in space.

Guglielmo Marconi was one of the first inventors to send telegraph signals through the air using radio waves.

Early developments

Radio developed from the theories and experiments of many people. In the 1830's, the scientists Joseph Henry and Michael Faraday discovered one of the first important ideas in the development of radio. Both men had experimented with **electromagnets**—temporary magnets formed when electric current flows through a wire or other material that transmits electricity. Most electromagnets consist of wire wrapped around an iron core.

Separately, Henry and Faraday each developed the theory that an electric current in one wire can produce a current in another wire, without the wires being connected. In 1864, the Scottish scientist James Clerk Maxwell helped explain this theory by suggesting the existence of invisible **electromagnetic waves** that travel at the speed of light. Electromagnetic waves are waves of energy made up of an electric and a magnetic field. During the late 1880's, the German scientist Heinrich Hertz did experiments that proved Maxwell's theory.

The Tesla coil

In 1891, an American inventor from Austria-Hungary named Nikola Tesla invented the Tesla coil. This device increases or decreases the strength of electric current that regularly reverses its direction. It is still an essential component of the equipment used to send out radio waves.

Orson Welles was a famed actor and director of radio series in the 1930's.

Between the 1920's to the early 1950's, radio broadcasting had much the same entertainment role as television has today. ❯

The first radio signals

Guglielmo Marconi was an Italian inventor who helped pioneer the use of radio as a modern form of communication. In 1895, Marconi combined earlier ideas with his own and sent the first radio communication signals through the air. In 1901, Marconi's radio equipment sent coded signals across the Atlantic Ocean from England to Newfoundland (now Newfoundland and Labrador), Canada.

The Golden Age of radio

Radio stations in the United States and other countries began regular broadcasts in the 1920's. Between 1925 and the early 1950's, radio was a major source of family entertainment. Every night, many families gathered in their living rooms to listen to comedies, adventure dramas, music, and other kinds of radio entertainment. The rise of television in the 1950's ended the Golden Age of radio broadcasting. People turned to TV for entertainment, and these kinds of shows all but disappeared from radio.

Wireless Technology

Today, many users of computers, cell phones, and other electronic devices use wireless technology to connect to the **Internet**. Wireless communication uses radio waves to send and receive information through air or space. This enables laptop computers and other electronic devices in relatively close proximity to transfer data without the use of wires.

Television is one of our most important means of communication. It brings images from around the world into millions of homes.

Early experiments

Television works by changing pictures and sounds from a scene into electronic signals. A television set receives these signals and turns them back into pictures and sounds.

Television became possible in the 1800's, when people learned how to send communication signals through the air as **electromagnetic waves.** The first radio operators sent coded signals through the air. By the early 1900's, operators could transmit words. Meanwhile, many scientists had experimented with transmitting pictures.

In 1929, a Russian-born American scientist named Vladimir K. Zworykin demonstrated the first completely electronic, practical television system.

In TV's early days, people who had no set often visited friends who had one just to watch television.

An experimental telecast of the late 1920's showed an image of the comic strip character Felix the Cat.

The first broadcasts

The first television broadcast was made in 1936 by the British Broadcasting Corporation (BBC) in the United Kingdom. In 1939, the National Broadcasting Company (NBC) made the first TV broadcast in the United States.

At first, telecasts in the United States reached only the Eastern Seaboard between Boston and Washington, D.C. But by 1951, they extended coast-to-coast. TV stations sprang up throughout the country. Entertainment, news, special events, and sports contests replaced the simple, largely experimental, shows.

In 1945, there were probably fewer than 10,000 television sets in the United States. This figure soared to about 6 million in 1950 and to almost 60 million by 1960.

Television today

Improvements in broadcasting and receiving equipment have helped provide much clearer television images than in the past. In TV's early days, all programs were telecast in black and white. Color television broadcasts began in 1953. Today, almost all programs are telecast in color.

Digital television represents one of the biggest changes in television since the introduction of color in the 1950's. In the 1990's and early 2000's, many broadcasters around the world began broadcasting digital television signals incorporating high-definition television (HDTV). HDTV is a type of digital television that produces extremely sharp images.

Television technology continues to improve. Some televisions can be combined with other devices and used to browse the **Internet** and to send and receive e-mail. In 2010, 3-D television sets were introduced to the market.

TV Facts

- A form of reality television began in the late 1940's with "Candid Camera." The show used hidden cameras to capture people responding to odd or surprising situations.

- The first televised presidential debates took place in 1960. U.S. presidential candidates John F. Kennedy and Richard M. Nixon faced off in a series of television debates before the American public.

- The Vietnam War (1957-1975) was sometimes called "the first war to be fought on television." Battle scenes from the war were regularly televised. Viewers also watched bitter debates over the war and demonstrations by war protesters.

Recent innovations in television include 3-D TV's that do not require the use of special glasses. ▼

Flying High

For thousands of years, people dreamed of flying. Today, millions of people depend on airplanes for swift travel across the globe. Spacecraft powered by rockets can even take people far beyond the boundaries of Earth.

The Wright Brothers made their first successful flight near Kitty Hawk, North Carolina, on December 17, 1903.

The Wright brothers

During the 1890's, Orville Wright and Wilbur Wright became interested in flying while operating their bicycle-manufacturing shop in Dayton, Ohio. The brothers knew that their flying machine needed a wing shape that would help lift it off the ground. They tried many shapes before finding the right one. On Decem-ber 17, 1903, Orville Wright became the first person to successfully fly an engine-driven, heavier-than-air machine.

By the 1930's, planes were carrying passengers across oceans. These first planes had propellers driven by piston engines. Pistons are short cylinders of metal fitting closely inside a tube or hollow cylinder. A piston engine burns gasoline to move the pistons back and forth. The motion of the pistons can then be converted into a circular motion, which can be used for power.

The first space shuttle mission began on April 12, 1981, with the launch of the Columbia. The shuttles were designed to blast off like a rocket, land like an airplane, and make up to 100 missions.

The jet engine

Engineers then tried producing a **jet** engine. This kind of engine releases a high-pressure stream of gas in the opposite direction of the vehicle, causing it to thrust forward. In 1939, the first successful jet plane flew in Germany. British and American jet planes followed in the early 1940's.

By the end of World War II (1939-1945), jets could fly faster than propeller-driven planes, but not as far. Engineers worked to improve the power and speed of jet planes, mainly for military purposes. Commercial jet airliners began service in the United Kingdom and the United States in the 1950's.

To the moon

Large, heavy spacecraft need a powerful booster rocket to launch them. Boosters burn fuel that gives off gases in bursts that push the spacecraft off the ground and into the air. When the spacecraft reaches a certain speed, it breaks free of Earth's gravity. A spacecraft fires a rocket again to increase its speed or to change direction.

After World War II, the United States and the Soviet Union built rockets for both military purposes and space research. In 1957, the Soviet Union launched Sputnik, the first **artificial satellite.** The Soviets also put the first person in space, when astronaut Yuri Gagarin (*YOOR ee gah GAHR ihn)* made a single orbit of Earth in 1961. In 1969, Apollo 11 American astronauts Neil Armstrong and Buzz Aldrin became the first human beings to set foot on the moon.

Rockets, spacecraft, computer and guidance systems, astronauts' equipment and spacesuits were all developed by scientists and engineers working together in teams. Today, scientists in the United States, Russia, Europe, Japan, and other countries work together to build space stations and plan future explorations in space.

The first commercial jet airliners began service during the 1950's.

Rocket Firsts

- War rockets were used during the 1800's. Some of these rockets had fins for guidance.

- In 1903, a Russian teacher named Konstantin Tsiolkovsky published the correct theory of rocket power.

- In 1926, the American scientist Robert H. Goddard launched a small liquid-propellant rocket that rose 184 feet (56 meters) into the air.

- During World War II, German scientists developed the V-2 guided missile. After the war, American and Soviet engineers used captured V-2 rockets for research.

- In 1957, the Soviet Union launched the first artificial satellite.

- In 1961, a Soviet rocket put the first astronaut, Major Yuri Gagarin, into orbit around Earth.

- In 1969, a Saturn V rocket sent America's Apollo 11 astronauts to the moon. Two astronauts made the first walk on the surface of the moon.

Computers have changed the way we work, learn, communicate, and play. Nearly every kind of organization throughout the world uses computers to conduct business.

The first computer

The computer is not the invention of one single person. Computers came from the ideas and inventions of many people over many years. These people were **engineers,** mathematicians, and scientists.

The first all-purpose computer was built in 1946. It was called ENIAC (Electronic Numerical Integrator And Computer). ENIAC was so big it filled an entire room.

Minichip marvels

The integrated circuit was one of the most important developments in computer technology. This tiny device controls electric signals. It can hold thousands of electronic parts on a paper-thin chip.

Two Americans—engineer Jack Kilby and scientist Robert Noyce—**patented** the first integrated circuits in 1959. By 1971, further work had produced the microprocessor, a "computer on a chip." This allowed computers to become even smaller and more powerful. Today, a computer part the size of a fingernail can do the same work as the original ENIAC.

Microsoft founders Bill Gates and Paul Allen introduced the Altair 8800 in 1975. Only electronics hobbyists bought these computers.

Steve Jobs revealed Apple's iPad in January 2010. The tablet computer has a touchscreen keyboard and works as an e-book reader, a music and video player, and a game console.

Personal computers

The first personal computer, the Altair, was introduced in 1975. But these computers had to be assembled, and they did not become widely popular. That same year, former schoolmates Bill Gates and Paul Allen founded Microsoft Corporation to develop programs for the Altair.

In 1976, two young American computer enthusiasts, Steven P. Jobs and Stephen G. Wozniak, founded Apple Computer, Inc. (now Apple Inc.). The next year, they introduced the Apple II personal computer. The Apple II was much less expensive than earlier computers. It was sold as an assembled unit, not as a kit. As a result, computers became available to people other than computer specialists and technicians.

In 1981, IBM entered the personal computer market with its PC. The machine was even more successful than the Apple II. Microsoft soon began to develop programs for the PC. Personal computers were purchased by small and medium-sized businesses that could not afford larger, more powerful computers or did not need the immense computing power that mainframes provided. Millions of individuals, families, and schools also bought personal computers. In 1984, Apple scored another success with the Macintosh, a powerful, easy-to-use desktop computer. In 1998, Apple hit another homerun with the iMac, which launched a series of "i" products, including the iPod in 2001 and iPad in 2010.

Computers today

As computer power has increased, so has computer speed. Meanwhile, the size and cost of computers has shrunk steadily even as computer functions and programs become more varied.

Getting to Know Bill

- Bill Gates wanted to be a scientist when he grew up. He excelled in mathematics and science in school.

- At the age of eight, Gates set out to read every volume of *The World Book Encyclopedia*. He made it to volume P before deciding he didn't have the patience to continue.

- Bill Gates was only 15 years old when he set up his first software company with Paul Allen. Five years later, he cofounded Microsoft. Microsoft is now the world's largest developer and publisher of software for personal computers.

The Internet

Today, people can look up the answer to a question within seconds. They can send text messages, photographs, and videos using computers or mobile devices. None of this would be possible without the Internet, a huge network of computers that connects many of the world's businesses, institutions, and individuals.

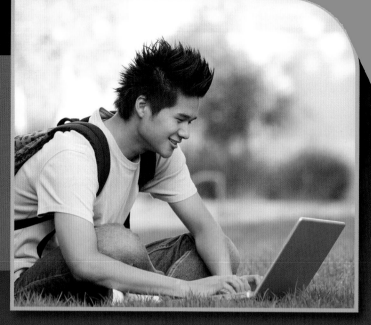

Some cities and universities have wireless technology "hubs" that allow users to access the Internet within a certain area.

The first computer networks

The **Internet** began to take shape in the late 1960's. The United States Department of Defense began investigating means of linking computer installations together so that their ability to communicate might withstand a war. Through its Advanced Research Projects Agency (ARPA), the Defense Department started ARPANet, a network of university and military computers.

Throughout the 1970's, ARPANet grew at a slow but steady pace. Computers in other countries began to join the network. Other networks came into existence as well. Soon, the collection of networks became known simply as the Internet.

One of the reasons for the slow growth of the early Internet was the difficulty of using the network. To access its information, users had to master complex series of programming commands that required either memorization or frequent reference to special manuals.

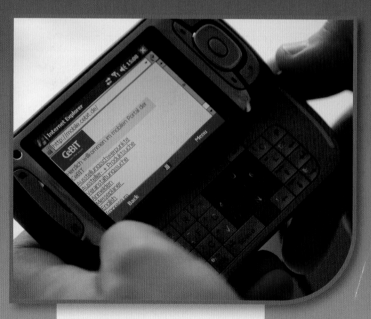

Smartphones enable people to access the Internet from nearly any location.

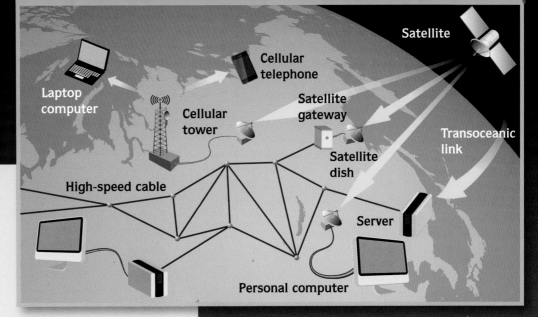

Many different types of equipment enable people to gain access to the Internet. High-speed communication lines, wireless **transmitters,** and **satellites** may all play a part in a single exchange of information between two computers via the Internet.

Image labels: Satellite, Cellular telephone, Laptop computer, Cellular tower, Satellite gateway, Transoceanic link, Satellite dish, High-speed cable, Server, Personal computer

The World Wide Web

The Internet's breakthrough to mass popularity occurred in 1991 with the arrival of the World Wide Web. The Web was developed by Tim Berners-Lee, a British computer scientist at the European Organization for Nuclear Research. The Web could deliver different media, such as text, pictures, sounds, and videos.

The programming language that the Web used, called HTML, made it far easier to link information from computers throughout the world. Users could jump easily from the resources of one computer to another, effortlessly following an information trail around the world.

The arrival of Web browsers in 1993 made using the Web and the Internet even easier, and brought about staggering growth in the Internet. A Web browser, such as Internet Explorer, Safari, or Mozilla Firefox, is a software package used to access locations on the World Wide Web.

The Internet today

New technologies continue to increase the importance of the Internet. Handheld computers and Internet-capable cellular telephones allow people to access the Internet from any location. Wireless networking technologies use radio waves to link a computer to the Internet.

Did You Know?

- *Internet* is short for "interconnected network of networks."

- The Internet and the World Wide Web are two different things. The Internet is a vast network of computers that links individuals and most of the world's businesses and institutions. The World Wide Web is part of the Internet. It delivers text, pictures, sounds, and videos from one computer to another all over the world.

The History of Inventions and Discoveries

People have made inventions and discoveries from earliest times to the present day. This list includes many of the most important ones. Notice how many inventions and discoveries have been made in the last 200 years.

Bronze arrowhead

The Ancient World

More than 2 million years ago People used flint tools.

About 1.5 million years ago People used fire.

About 11,000 B.C. People made pottery from clay.

About 9000 B.C. People had become farmers.

About 3500 B.C. The wheel was invented and the Sumerians developed the first known system of writing. At about this time, people learned to make bronze by melting copper and tin together, and to fire bricks in an oven.

3000's B.C. The Egyptians developed basic geometry and surveying techniques. They discovered how to make sails, and learned how to build boats out of planks of wood. The Egyptians made irrigation devices to bring water to fields, and used a 365-day calendar.

About 2000 B.C. The sundial, the oldest known instrument for telling the time, was invented.

About 1400 B.C. Iron began to replace bronze for tools and weapons.

About 1000 B.C. The Chinese flew the first kites.

About 400 B.C. Democritus (Greece) taught that all matter was made of tiny atoms.

400's B.C. Hippocrates (Greece) showed that diseases have only natural, not supernatural, causes.

300's B.C. Aristotle (Greece) formed theories in many areas of physics.

200's B.C. Archimedes (Greece) discovered the law of the lever and pulley, and the laws of the behavior of liquids.

A.D. 100's Ptolemy (a Greek living in North Africa) proposed that Earth is the center of the universe. By this time, the Romans had developed cement and concrete, and made the best roads of their time. The Chinese had invented paper.

A.D. 500 to 1500

1100's Alchemy, a major source of chemical knowledge, reached western Europe from the Arab lands. The Chinese were first to use the magnetic compass, by about 1100.

1200's Gunpowder rockets were invented in China.

About 1300 Shipbuilders in northern Europe introduced the stern rudder, another Chinese invention.

About 1350 Cannon were first used in war.

About 1440 Printing with movable type was invented in Europe.

Late 1400's In Italy, Leonardo da Vinci studied anatomy, **astronomy,** botany, and geology.

1500 to 1700

1519-1522 The first voyage around the world was completed by sailors of Ferdinand Magellan's expedition.

1500's Ambroise Paré (France) introduced new surgical techniques.

1543 Vesalius (Flanders, now Belgium) published the first scientific study of human anatomy.

1543 Copernicus (Poland) wrote that Earth and the planets revolve in circles around the sun.

Late 1500's Tycho Brahe (Denmark) observed the motions of the planets.

About 1590 The compound microscope was invented.

1608 The telescope was invented.

Early 1600's In Italy, Galileo set up experiments to find the true laws of falling bodies, and discovered many principles of mechanics. He was one of the first scientists to use a telescope to study the sky.

1628 William Harvey (Britain) published his book on blood circulation.

1640's Blaise Pascal (France) invented a mechanical calculator.

1660's Robert Boyle (Ireland) taught that theories must be supported by careful experiments—the basis of modern science. He also set out laws relating gas pressure to volume.

1663 The first drawings of cells appeared in a book by Robert Hooke (Britain), who pioneered the use of the microscope and discovered the new world of cells.

1670's Anton van Leeuwenhoek (Holland) discovered microscopic forms of life **(bacteria).**

1687 Isaac Newton (Britain) published his laws of motion.

1690 Christiaan Huygens (Holland) published a wave theory of light.

1698 Thomas Savery (Britain) built a **steam engine** for pumping water.

Galileo Galilei

1700 to 1800

1712 Thomas Newcomen (Britain) built an improved **steam engine.**

1735 Carolus Linnaeus (Sweden) classified plants and animals according to their structural similarities, laying the foundation for modern scientific classification.

1752 Benjamin Franklin (America) proved that lightning was electricity.

1766 Henry Cavendish (Britain) identified the gas hydrogen as an element.

1769-1770 Nicholas-Joseph Cugnot (France) built two steam-powered road vehicles.

1770's Carl Scheele (Sweden) and Joseph Priestley (Britain) discovered oxygen. James Watt (Britain) developed improved steam engines. New machines for spinning and weaving textiles were invented.

1777 By this date, Antoine Lavoisier (France) had discovered the nature of combustion or burning. He also proved that water consists of hydrogen and oxygen.

1781 William Herschel (Britain) discovered the planet Uranus, the first of the two most distant planets to be identified. The other six planets had been known since ancient times.

1783 The Montgolfier brothers (France) made the first flight in a hot-air balloon.

1790's Count Volta (Italy) made the first battery.

1793 Eli Whitney (United States) made his cotton gin.

1796 Edward Jenner (Britain) gave the first **vaccination,** against smallpox.

Charles Darwin

1800 to 1900

1801 Richard Trevithick (Britain) developed a four-wheeled steam carriage. Robert Fulton (United States) built a working submarine.

1803 John Dalton (Britain) proposed his atomic theory about the structure of matter.

1807 Robert Fulton built the first commercially successful steamboat.

1818 Britain launched the first all-iron sailing ship.

Early 1820's Charles Babbage (Britain) began to develop mechanical computers.

1825 The first public steam-hauled railroad began operating, in Britain.

1826 The first photograph was taken, in France.

1830 Charles Lyell (Britain) showed that Earth has changed slowly through the ages.

1831 Cyrus McCormick (United States) built the first mechanical reaper.

Early 1830's Michael Faraday (Britain) and Joseph Henry (United States) independently proved a relationship between electricity and magnetism.

1836 The first screw propellers were developed to drive steamboats.

1837 Samuel Morse (United States) demonstrated his electric **telegraph.**

1838-1839 Matthias Schleiden and Theodor Schwann (Germany) proposed that the cell is the basic unit of life.

1840's First use of ether, the first practical **anesthetic.**

1845 *The Great Britain,* designed by Isambard Kingdom Brunel, became the first propeller-driven ship to travel across the Atlantic Ocean.

Mid-1800's Louis Pasteur (France) founded modern microbiology, with his studies of germs as the causes of disease. Gregor Mendel (Austria) discovered the basic laws of heredity, devising the theory of genes from studies of pea plants.

1856 Sir William Perkin (Britain) made the first synthetic (artificial) dye.

The first motor carriage

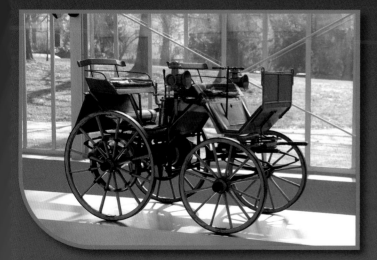

1859 Charles Darwin (Britain) set forth his theory of evolution in *On the Origin of Species.*

1860 Jean Joseph Étienne Lenoir (France) **patented** the internal-combustion engine.

1864 James Clerk Maxwell (Britain) published his **electromagnetic** theory of light.

1869 Dmitri Mendeleyev (Russia) published his periodic table of the elements.

1870 Celluloid, the first synthetic plastic material to be sold widely, was invented by John W. and Isaiah Hyatt (United States).

1876 Alexander Graham Bell, a Scot living in the United States, invented the telephone.

1877 Thomas A. Edison (United States) invented the phonograph.

1879 Edison and Joseph Swan (Britain) independently invented the electric light bulb.

1885 Gottlieb Daimler and Karl Benz (Germany) built the first automobiles.

1895 Wilhelm Roentgen (Germany) discovered X rays. The first public showing of motion pictures took place in Paris, France. The first radio signals were sent by Marconi (Italy).

1896 Antoine Becquerel (France) discovered natural radioactivity.

1897 The first steam-turbine ship, the *British Turbinia,* was demonstrated.

1898 Marie and Pierre Curie (Poland/France) discovered the element radium. Marie Curie became famous for her research on radioactivity.

1900 to the Present

1901 **Mass production** of cars began in the United States. Radio signals were sent across the Atlantic Ocean for the first time.

1903 Orville and Wilbur Wright (United States) made the world's first airplane flight.

1905 Albert Einstein (Germany) published his special theory of relativity, offering new ways of thinking about space and time. In 1915, Einstein announced his general theory of relativity explaining the effects of gravity.

1907 Paul Cornu (France) built a helicopter that flew but was not developed.

1909 Bakelite, an early plastic, was invented by Leo Baekeland (Belgium).

1920's Edwin Hubble (United States) discovered other galaxies. Frozen foods were invented.

Late 1920's Movies with synchronized sound replaced silent movies.

1928 Alexander Fleming (Britain) discovered penicillin, the first antibiotic drug.

1929 Electronic television was demonstrated for the first time.

1930 The **jet** engine was invented by Frank Whittle (Britain). The first jet-engine plane flew in Germany in 1939.

1931 Karl Jansky pioneered the radio telescope.

1930's Four important plastics—acrylics, nylon, polystyrene, and polyvinyl chloride (PVC or vinyl)— came into use.

Mid-1930's Radar was developed. Much early work on radar was done by Robert Watson-Watt (Britain).

Late 1930's The ballpoint pen was invented.

1938 The photocopier was invented by Chester Carlson (United States).

1942 In the United States, Enrico Fermi and his team achieved the first controlled nuclear chain reaction.

1945 The first atomic bombs were exploded. Nuclear power plants began generating electricity in the 1950's.

1946 The world's first electronic computer began working (United States).

Steve Jobs (right) and Steve Wozniak

Inventions and Discoveries

1947 The transistor was invented (United States).

1953 James Watson (United States) and Francis Crick (Britain) proposed a model of the molecular structure of deoxyribonucleic acid (DNA), the chemical that carries instructions that tell living things how to develop and work.

1954 The first successful organ transplant, of a kidney, was performed in the United States.

1956 Videotape recording was invented.

1957 The Soviet Union launched the first **artificial satellite.**

1959 The modern form of the air cushion vehicle or hovercraft was invented.

1960 Theodore Maiman (United States) built the first laser.

1961 Soviet cosmonaut Yuri Gagarin became the first person to orbit Earth in space.

1960's Communications satellites made worldwide television broadcasts possible.

1969 The U.S. spacecraft Apollo 11 landed the first astronauts on the moon.

1971 The Soviet Salyut 1 was the first manned orbiting space station.

1976 Two U.S. Viking space probes landed on Mars.

1980's Small, powerful computers became popular for home and school use, as well as in business and industry. The camcorder (a video camera and recorder in one unit) became available.

1981 The United States launched the first space shuttle.

1986 The U.S. space probe Voyager 2 flew past the planet Uranus, and on to Neptune, which it reached in 1989.

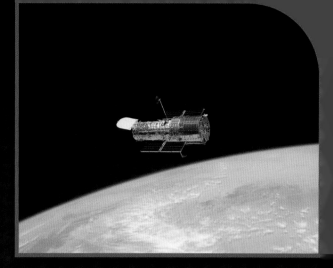

The Hubble Space Telescope

1990 The Hubble Space Telescope began studying the universe, from its orbit around Earth.

1990's More people used mobile cellular phones, CD's and CD-ROM's, and e-mail. The invention of the World Wide Web, and the browsers that made it easily accessible, made the **Internet** easier to use. Researchers expanded our knowledge of heredity and the use of genetic **engineering.**

2000's Smartphones become widely available. Car manufacturers begin mass-producing hybrid vehicles.

2004 The first commercial maglev (magnetic levitation) rail system began operations in Shanghai, China.

2007 The International Astronomical Union (IAU) created the category of dwarf planets and assigned Pluto to that category.

Glossary

anesthetic a drug that causes a loss of feeling in part or all of the body.

artificial satellite a human-made object that continuously orbits Earth or some other body in space.

astronomer; astronomy a person who studies astronomy; the science of the sun, moon, planets, stars, and all other celestial bodies.

bacteria single-celled organisms that can only be seen using a microscope.

civilization a society highly developed in its systems of government, agriculture, arts, and sciences.

electromagnet a piece of iron enclosed in a coil of wire. When an electric current passes through the wire, the iron turns magnetic.

electromagnetic wave a wave of energy made up of an electric and a magnetic field, generated when an electric charge moves back and forth or is accelerated.

engineer; engineering a person who plans and builds engines, machines, roads, bridges, canals, or the like; the use of science to design structures, machines, and products.

immunity resistance to disease.

Industrial Revolution a period in the late 1700's and early 1800's when the development of industries brought great change to many parts of the world.

Internet a vast network of computers that connects many of the world's businesses, institutions, and individuals.

irrigate to supply land with water by using ditches, by flooding, or by sprinkling.

jet a fast stream of liquid, steam, or gas sent through a small opening by strong pressure.

locomotive a machine that moves trains on railroad tracks. It is sometimes called a railroad engine.

mass production the making of goods in large quantities, especially by machinery and with division of labor.

navigate to sail, manage, or steer (a ship, aircraft, or rocket) on a course or to a destination.

patent (n.) a legal right given to an inventor, protecting a new invention from being copied by others; (v.) to get a patent for.

satellite see *artificial satellite.*

steam engine an engine that is operated by the energy of expanding steam.

telegraph a system or equipment for sending messages in code through electrical wires.

transmitter a part of a radio, telephone, telegraph, or television broadcasting system that sends out signals.

vaccine; vaccination a mixture containing weak or dead germs given to people or animals to protect them from the disease that those germs can cause; the act, practice, or process of giving a vaccine.

Books

American Women Inventors by Carol Ann Camp (Enslow Publishers, 2004)

Arab Science and Invention in the Golden Age by Anne Blanchard and Emmanuel Cerisier (Enchanted Lion Books, 2008.)

Galileo Galilei: Inventor, Astronomer and Rebel by Michael White (Blackbirch Press, 1999)

Ideas That Changed the World by Julie Ferris (DK Publishing, Inc., 2010)

The Real McCoy: The Life of an African-American Inventor by Wendy Towle and Wil Clay (Scholastic, 1993)

So You Want to Be an Inventor? by Judith St. George and David Small (Philomel Books, 2002)

Thomas A. Edison: The World's Greatest Inventor by Anna Sproule (Blackbirch Press, 2000)

Who Was Ben Franklin? by Dennis B. Fradin and John O'Brien (Grosset & Dunlap, 2002)

Women Invent: Two Centuries of Discoveries That Have Shaped Our World by Susan Casey (Chicago Review Press, 1997)

Websites

Exploring Leonardo
http://www.mos.org/sln/leonardo/

This site from the Museum of Science includes an Inventor's Workshop, where Leonardo da Vinci's visionary sketches are paired up with modern-day technology.

The Galileo Project
http://galileo.rice.edu

Follow the life and work of Galileo Galilei on this site, which also includes a library of additional resources.

Inventors and Inventions
http://www.enchantedlearning.com/inventors/

Inventors and inventions from A to Z are available in this online database, which also contains sections on inventions by women and African Americans.

Museum of Ancient Inventions
http://www.smith.edu/hsc/museum/ancient_inventions/

This online museum, created by Smith College, features images and descriptions of ancient inventions, from Aztec calendar wheels to a 2000-year-old battery.

The Lemelson Center for the Study of Invention and Innovation
http://invention.smithsonian.org/home

Inventions past and present are featured on this website, which also includes the MIND database of science- and invention-related collections.

Lighting a Revolution
http://americanhistory.si.edu/lighting/

Follow the steps of invention as Edison's light bulb makes way for modern, energy-efficient lighting.

National Inventors' Hall of Fame
http://www.invent.org/hall_of_fame/1_0_0_hall_of_fame.asp

The National Inventors' Hall of Fame website contains biographies for inventors who have made extraordinary contributions to science and technology.

A Science Odyssey: Doctor Over Time
http://www.pbs.org/wgbh/aso/tryit/doctor/

Describe your symptoms to doctors from different eras, and learn how inventions and discoveries advanced medicine throughout the 20th century.

The Top Ten African-American Inventors
http://teacher.scholastic.com/activities/bhistory/inventors

Brilliant minds from George Washington Carver to Madam C.J. Walker are profiled on this website, along with their inventions and innovations.

The Wright Brothers: The Invention of the Aerial Age
http://www.nasm.si.edu/wrightbrothers/index_full.cfm

This online exhibit from the National Air and Space Museum features interactive experiments, timelines, and information on the lives of Wilbur and Orville Wright.